Blue POSITIVE

Blue POSITIVE

Martha Silano

STEEL TOE BOOKS
BOWLING GREEN, KENTUCKY

ISBN 0-9743264-2-9

Steel Toe Books
Department of English
135 Cherry Hall
Western Kentucky University
1 Big Red Way
Bowling Green, KY 42101-3576

Table of Contents

IV.
Forgetfulness the Great Bronchial Tree from Which I'm Swinging

V.
My Body Will Run with the Weeds Some Day

To Langdon
for seeing me through the darkness
and to Riley and Ruby
for light

Blue Positive

To begin I need to tell you about Phoenix, who's telling me he's so hungry
he could eat twenty sumo wrestlers, diapers and all. I need to tell you
about these puke-yellow walls, about Ms. Potthoff, how she shines

in this cluttered, chalk-choked room like the Iowa sun in July, cares
for these kids like they care about their class pet Lizzy,
a leopard gecko; I need you to see Christabel's

two inch navy blue fingernails, who wrote *for even your father
was once a stranger*, also smiling Myra, who tells us
Celtic music's like holding a cat, like taking

her first bath, like her brother and sister being born.
I need to take off this scratchy sweater, put on
my old gray sweatshirt, fraying at the seams,

the zipper about to go. I need to tell you about the white boot
that used to be my sister's, then mine, then my little brother's
as he hopped home, one foot bare, one still-warm boot

stuck in the neighbor's drifting snow. Arnold says it's like the colors
of a Mexican sky, a tarpon's glistening fin, while Jamar,
Jamar says we should all have, like the dog

whose owner always gives him the last piece of poppy-seed cake,
a quiet place to lie down. Listening, I hear the waves
off the coast of St. Ives, where gannets, common

as pasties, stretched every inch of their seventy-two inch spans.
Listening, I need to take you to the Seep Lakes late, very late
on the night of the Leonids, my son with a cold,

so in all the photos, where my best friend Lisa Sylvester
said an angel had shushed me, had shushed us all,
that glistening, which is why I must tell you

of Dr. Lydia Adler's gloved and sterile hands, how I slid out
blue, but blue positive; my mother's blood
the rain; if we could see it but we can't,

the sky, Ayla says, isn't crying; the sky never cries.
Our burdens are small, or just the right size.
I wore a red and black corduroy jumper,

in a lavender dress, sipped wine—a little of hers,
a little of theirs, like those seeping lakes,
seeping into mine.

I.

If You Want a Girl to Grow Up Gentle,
Lace Her Tight

I Never Wanted to Travel Through Time

Until I spilled a plate of beans and rice with hot sauce
into a customer's lap. Until I hastily misconstrued
the distance of my side view mirror
from the neighbor's fence,

sheared the mirror off like an ear of corn from the stalk.
When the plane you're in suddenly loses
lift, what else but to wish for the chance
to leave from C7,

not the disastrous C8. Never mind it was heading
for Saginaw, better than the nowhere soon
to be strewn with luggage blown to bits.
But to go back

to my kindergarten graduation—the pink-with-yellow-polka-dot dress,
a grocery bag's bottom dangling a crepe paper tassel,
to my father's "you did it!"— I'd live each day
with the look on the face of the man

who'd never return to Bandoleone's again, pay each week
his dry cleaning bill, look, for the rest of my life,
carefully over my shoulder, slowly,
slowly backing up.

Sprinklers of the Western World

there were the feathery fronds slow motion arcs bent-in-the-wind
    weeping willows
pitter-patter onto blossoming lilacs the favorite aunt who'd call
I'm out back on the chaise come on over

your favorite suit bleached lightest blue softest cotton handed down
from Candy to Suzie to Patty to Annie to you
beds of bleeding hearts

to run through to stick your whole head in two dozen streams
two dozen perfect pee holes to sit on block all but one
see how far it shot to drink from to lift to spray
and spray your shiny body
till it shook

there was the brown twirling spider happily squeaking
turned down low dribbling liquid feelers
full blast stopped with the touch
of a foot

Donald Duck and his candy stripe stick a weepy sparkler
from a green plastic ring a hundred static jets
no time for the grass
so so much mud

fifteen first heat first love walking him home you ran together
through every one under the wettest
kissed

the good ones spat a great distance
stream like a finger pointing
machine gun green
tsk tsk tsk tsk

dawn on an Iowa golf course topsoil cooled bedrock's mystery
drifting through asleep in your bag till a throat-clearing
sssspppptt sssspppptt full-on spurts sending you running

the not-exactly one in Bath which brings back all the others

water gurgling over coppery brick

steam and sulfur tempting ...

Ingredients

In one ear the crunch of *kapusta*—in the other the sizzle
of *bacala*. Through one nostril the deep, dark sting

of hot olive oil meeting garlic—through the other the steam
of cheddar cheese suffusing mashed potato peaks.

Some nights our burps told tales of *halushki*—
egg and flour plopped into swirling water,

then fried with buttery cabbage unfurling
past Poland, past Austria-Hungary, all the way back

to Mother Russia. Some nights the basil in *pasta siciliana*
sweetened our breath till dawn—our *sogni dori* green fields

skirting the Adriatic. Surely some of what they cooked
commingled—garlic-laden kielbasa, *galumpki* swimming

in a thick tomato sauce—but mostly what sautéed or steamed
married only completely in their children,

the four of us who entered their kitchen—little rumbling Etnas,
hollow perogies longing to be filled—who raised our glasses—*Salute!*—

to the bulka and to provolone, to all things *schmatzhnee* and *dolce*,
who left each night, a few flecks of pepper, a sprig of parsley,

still clinging to our teeth.

This is Not the Last Poem about Pears

and certainly not the first,
but I'm not talking
about D'Anjous, Comices,
Boscs, the ones you find
at a Safeway or a Food Lion
while under Muzak's spell,
pears which are sometimes sweet
like a kiss on the lips after many kisses
on the cheek, but more often not—
are like gnawing on the branch of a willow.
No. I'm talking about a pear from a tree
in your own yard, where rain, sun, and wind,
the occasional, inadvertent stumble
of a spider or an ant are all that has touched it.
And, at the very beginning, the petals,
on a rainy, or sunny, or windy day
which fall all at once like laundry
fresh from the spinning wash.
When they fall they leave behind
hundreds of parasols not unlike
the ones you saw as you gazed into pond water
under a microscope. Over the summer,
whether you notice or not,
they swell to miniature blowfish
but your father says, each time you ask,
not yet, so while rodents, bees, birds, worms...
you wait till he pulls in the drive and,
instead of heading straight for a nap,
joins you, picks one up—his tired body holding
the scent of machinery overworked—
looks it over, points to the one place not
worm-riddled, squirrel-gnawed,
hornet-bored, grackle-pecked:
Here, try that. It could've been mealy.
You could have swallowed
thorax, stinger, rotting flesh.
Instead your mouth is honored,
in a single bite, by a tiny planet
sweetened by a father's
immeasurable sacrifice.

Mother of Peace

but no quiet—
Puccini, Patsy Cline,
Some Enchanted Evening,
effervescing from unstoppable lips,
the unpieced quilt—
Texas Troubles—
tabled twenty years
as she presses her foot
to the Singer's pedal, inching along
the rickrack of a hooded dress
while I doze on the bed,
intermittent surges stirring.
Mother of wisdom—
vinegar/lemon in lieu of Windex,
jelly most un-petroleum.
Matriarch of markets—
resurrecting last week's beets,
overseer of kugel, *kapusta*, kale.
Queen of the tooth-chipping
biscotti, triple baked.

Mother of pizzicato
and pasta, the war
against throw away.
Resilient reassurer,
religiously renegade,
refuser of old age.

Little red hen gone global.
Teeny tiny woman with her teeny tiny bone
shirking her osteo-hunch. Woman who lived
in the pastel-pink, snakeskin pump.

Mother of *right to the moon* and *don't you dare,*
I'll give ya's and *so's your Aunt Lizzies,*
serving, on Easter, all Arkansas,
then cracking hickories for the Christmas loaf,
clues to the Sunday puzzle, digging around

for the root of nasturtium, the why
of Silano. Mother of peace
but no quiet. Dress
I wriggled into,
never took off.

If You Want a Girl to Grow up Gentle, Lace Her Tight

Bound this way I am anything but boundless I'm so bound I'm bound to feel
and I'm feeling out of bounds but I'm a believer in being bound
for better things—wide wide highway-bound six or eight
or sixteen lanes a wide berth for a wide-bodied plane
tarmack runway blue landing lights marking
the boundary between gentle
and gruff between docile
and tough the calm
where the windy
stubble the wild
desert prickly
begins
they want
my waist thin
as a stalk of bamboo
the wind whispers through
want it narrow like the narrowest spot
in a wide riverbed diked getty-ed pier-ed
contained—end to spilling fingers reaching
plains they want it channeled dredged want the water
over there to stay there it is lacy this tightening it is the opposite the very
opposite of unraveling it is quite the opposite of 26-foot swells of cresting and lapping

My Words

I never liked *pachyderm*, especially when I learned elephants are anything
but thick-skinned. Ditto to the dowdily galumphing *dromedary*
with its root in *dromad*, Greek for swift.

Ones I never considered memorable or strange—
bubble, banana, anemone—bloomed
when my son began to use them

to describe falling snow, a crescent moon,
a cockatiel's plume. Plum is a terrible
word for a perfect fruit, *summer*

beautiful as the cold and empty beach we stroll nine months
of the year. I like *gingivitis* and *gaggle*. *Gizzard*, too—
it must be all that ga ga goo—must be,

if not primal, crib-al, must harken back to days
pre-list, pre-who-is-this-this-
in-the-mirror? Pre-must-do.

I wanted *gourds* and *ghouls*; I wanted *gargantuan galas*,
gherkins galore, but really what I wanted
was that somersaultingly salty

source, to return to a time when my skin
was transparent, when water
was my word.

II.

Salvaging Just Might Lead to Salvation

People Are Doing It As We Speak

Near that pumpkin patch just off the interchange in Fall City.
In a swamp beside a Gumbo Limbo in Boca Raton. Opening

their Kama Sutras, saddling up for the Congress of the Cow.
Storming fire stations, eyeing the hook and ladder,

clanging the bells. At home, they're fixing to glue the kids
to Bob the Builder, climbing (quickly) the bedroom stairs,

before the youngest unleashes a dozen Tampax,
swirls a string in each ecstatic hand ("Look, mama—I'm fishing!").

With their carpet beaters, with their spatulas, they're positioning themselves
for the Splitting of a Bamboo. Like two wing-to-wing silvery blues,

they've dreamed up a new use for the golden onions,
for the skewered, roasting bird. Though they can't quite figure out

Perfuming the Garden, though the video's gone fuzzy, they're down
on all fours, not quite gone berserk but good enough.

I'll Never be Dorianne Laux at the Laundromat

eyeing the woman who's eyeing the guy
in blue silk jogging shorts *I want to lie down*

in the dry dung I want to hump every moving thing
but that's not to say I don't notice

the man at the Y who swaggers by my Lifecycle
banana in one hand other down his

blue silk jogging shorts massaging his bum
till he's almost breathing garlic down

my sweaty neck (I bet you taste better than a bear claw
better than teriyaki sauce sucked from beneath a fingernail)

till I'm thinking a good foot shorter but Greeky
like my Portland man's quarter acre of sun-ripened chest hair...

not to say I haven't in the space of a week
dreamed I'm fucking not one but two

of my colleagues no I'll probably never sing the praises
of my crotch-stained underwear (no way

would I think to call that color *honey*) but all around me
the scent of daffodils all around me desire devouring the leaves

like I'm about to devour an entire pound of A&P Bing cherries
the ones my father what the hell happened I just wanted

a handful don't tell me you went and ate them all?

My Man with his Fly Reel Eyes

After Andre Breton

My man with his fly reel eyes
Pale morning dun desire

My man's hip-wader heat
Gravel-in-the-shallows drive

My man with his Yakima Canyon shoulders
Sagebrush brow

My man's fingerling tongue
Biceps smooth as skipping stones

My man with his sockeye sperm
Trunk of ponderosa

My man's teeth the snow-fresh tracks
of cougar—cougar scream & cougar silence

My man's Frenchmen Coulee hands
My man the hawk with a snake in its mouth

My man the trout growing larger
My man skunked—his cattail want

My man the 40-mile-an-hour gust
a tarp set free from rocks

Traveler's Lament

Should we have stayed at home and dreamed of here? Where should we be today?

—Elizabeth Bishop

I miss the man who sells us wine, suggests
the Covey Run,

Rainbow Grocery's neon orange tennis ball
tangerine stacks.

I miss the flower shop with its bundles of African Daisies,
Queen Anne's Lace.

I miss our street, gossamer blossoms stuck like unlucky insects
to windshields, headlights.

I even miss the neighbor's pick-up turning over, at six am,
like twenty Hoovers and a leaf blower,

clang of dumpster lid. Futility of sweeping sunflower hulls
from the walk,

the mailman bringing (politely, almost daily) more and more
of nothing.

I miss lugging the trash to the curb in a robe
about to slip open.

The hot water tank we easily emptied
each time we made love in the tub.

To Know a Flower

One must be prepared to know the meaning
of *mucronate* ("tipped with a sharp point"), of *tegules*
("bracts surrounding the heads of composites").
To speak of flowers, one must have an openness
to the axillary and the cymose, to the retrosely barbed,
to even the cleistogamous. When you want to say pit,
say drupe. When you want to say *dotted,* say *punctate.*
When you want to describe a cluster, call it *fascicled.*
Perhaps you are thinking *but I just want to pick it,*
I just want to sniff. All of us have wanted, at times,
the same, to live—for an hour, for a day—without
scrutiny, or else with the kind of scrutiny that veers away
from the Latinate, away from Adam's job and closer
to Basho's. But to know a flower, you will need
a magnifying glass. Aim it on the grouping
of light green fruits (*achenes*) sitting inside
the corolla. Examine their beaks. Are they straight?
Recurved? Flattened? Glabrous? Take a second look
at the leaves: Shallowly toothed? Deeply crenate?
Round-tipped? Retuse? Now you're approaching

the kind of knowing which should lead you
to questions like these: would we be considered
pubescent (hairy or downy) or glabrate (approaching
smoothness)? Are we stellate (star-like, spreading
like the rays of a star)? Connate and conniving, doomed
to decumbence, or are we swinging free? Are our lungs not
papilionoeceous? Which should not (which does not)
negate the urge to abandon all of one's carefully copied
vocabulary, the nouns and adjectives of size and shape,
degrees of stickiness, of appendages' lengths
and offer a lover a swish, beneath the nose, of buttercup,
which should in no way lessen the need to lie in a field of them,
of American bistort and Indian paintbrush, of alpine lupine.

Salvaging Just Might Lead to Salvation

so when you come home there's a tickle in my throat what
should I take is there tea? Could you make it with honey? Could you
bring me an aspirin a pillow all the New Yorkers? Could you turn up the heat
so we almost choke? & the remote? Could you stick a Coke in the freezer? I do

& when I come home with a headache the size of New Hampshire
you go oh my sweet sweet square root of three
my tikka masala poppadum chutney-dipped
let me get you a patch of blue a stratocumulus don't move

so when you come home at noon in a suit going yeah I know I know
I got fired I'm all ears those bastards! they don't know
who they're losing but didn't you say you weren't anywhere close
to a window & how about those cubicles

so when I come home with a nasty note from a student *you're not
fostering my learning* you tell me there's a present for me on the couch
& when I get there it's a what-really-counts-is-letting-them-stand-
in-another-person's-tossed-from-a-speeding-car-and-sitting-on-the-freeway's shoes

which also means after months of *we'll let you knows* and *we'll call yous*
on the day I say honey maybe you should call the folks
at Parker Personnel you get the job & it's the right one
the one you've always wanted & when you pop
the cork unbelievably I catch it all the dogs convening
a crazy canine chorus praising perseverance luck

which means when some god of the classroom lets me slip
into improv zone & I'm on a roll & there's this buzz
and they're getting it! they're getting what it means
to have all been to Auburn but not one of them to Fife
that they all hated their 2nd grade teachers but love baked beans
Lyle Lovett windy nights you know to bring me not only
#2 pencil yellow African daisies exam-book blue
forget-me-nots and fresh as a brand new roster
lilies but to tell all the guys at the poker table
I'm the best teacher in all King County

which means when my card slides out from the little slot WE CANNOT
PROCESS YOUR ACCOUNT TRY AGAIN LATER you're ready
with your card & when the money you made tagging fish
in the Bering Sea dries up and disappears I pay
for the yellow finns jalapeños tortillas turtle beans
& God forbid we need to go back on food-stamps
I'll stand in line at DSHS
Silano? I can almost taste it while you head off to Our Lady
of the Dunes melt the Velveeta till it's almost brie

which means we've stopped keeping track of who paid for what
who bought table skillet spoon who'll fork it up for the rent
who scratched broke dirtied tangled what focus instead
on averting fights fending them off
like nasty germs that are hell on a throat on a life

& when really we want to say *you're selfish you're so fucking selfish* I'm
selfish but if you'd wipe the counters put out the trash
or on the one nice thing they did that day week month
or even yes a fight a good one real juicy not lugging up
88-year-old phlegm but new stuff like don't tell me
when I'm bloated or starting every
other raging sentence *you*

& now and then so horrible it ends in tears me of course wailing
almost screaming you're the wrong person I made a mistake
I hate you I hate you but because you're there to hold me
a miracle my pea brain *maybe he really really does love me won't*

leave which doesn't mean he won't which doesn't mean
this way of taking care is for everyone or only for hets
or like I'm advocating some kind of morality
Anita Bryant fresh-squeezed homophobic
takeover or even that single people
are inherently unhappy mistaken
or downright lost

but that maybe we're meant like great-crested grebes mouths dripping
slimy weeds lifting erect or the bird of paradise that clears on the forest floor
a place to lift glinting wings to waltz twirl leap to land on a mate
he'll keep though yes it's oversimplifying anthropomorphizing
is not the way a red-winged blackbird colony operates

but if we're to trust the eyes and ears of anthropologists & scientists
over 90% of birds & humans are monogamous though I'm not 100% sure
they're including the Choctaw, Crow, Cherokee, Creek, Pawnee, Minitari,
& Arichara for whom the husband weds not just his wife

but aunts & nieces too kinship increasingly matted a woven mesh
precariously dangling not too unlike a bushtit nest till
this situation ends in IX (MB = B; MBW = BW) for any "a" is MB
though I bet it makes sense if it's all you know
like asking Emily Post
or the tribal elders

though it probably isn't true for every stomped on wine glass
borrowed or blue for every groped for garter tossed bouquet
sweetheart neckline Bertha collar or leg-of-mutton sleeve
there's a Moulay Ismail emperor of Morocco
siring 888 children from upwards of 200 wives
or the Tiwi nubile whose privates are poked
with a spear her future son-in-law
strokes hugs calls wife in this way marrying
all her unborn daughters

which means there's a chance you too might want someone
who'll buy more Kleenex tell you your tea is steeped shirt's
wrinkled tag's hanging out who swipes with licked finger
the ketchup from your cheek
who tells you my you're looking pale
knows how to raise
your drooping head

though I know you might be asking *marriage?! are you fucking kidding?
I just want some pussy!* which I don't blame you for at all especially
since there's a strong argument we're more like the forgivably
polygamous lion than a bunch of birds

a case to be made for a male to spread his seed
which is not to say every woman
craves monogamy

no matter how much our behavior resembles hornbills hoopoes
meercats cobras or moral owls I'm not about to tell you marriage
is easy or difficult or a hocus pocus fantasy only breeders want or know
not about to tell you it's for you

girls traded for coconuts chariots shields yams all of it resting
on capture hope-chests painstaking lace I'd almost say resist it
in homage to all those wasted lives all those hours
filling trousseaux before a father could breathe
a relief-ful sigh

I'd almost say stay single don't get stuck
like my grandmother says
washing some guy's
shorts

except I've always been drawn to the scraggliest plant on the shelf
leggy zucchini contorted delphinium mangiest chard
to fixing what just might have a second life
can't stand not trying to resurrect
a broken fan into could I?
a hotdog grill?

to taking a heap of a '61 Caddy spray-painted gold
half-reclaimed by Ozark mud
digging the damn thing out.

Define Medical Terminology and Conditions Associated with Conception

let's just say right now it's a wonder
sperm & egg found a way to fuse at all
that godforsakenly cold and drizzly day
gravelly jerky mud-puddled rutted all-too-jolting ride
icy bike seat jutting my miracled mound
for anything close to fertilization
lull and bob of a zygote (23 his, 23 mine)
though I must admit I never understood
Miss Barbieri's *oogenesis*
which sounded more
like someone about to come
than *formation of a haploid ovum*

Normally Tiger Mountain's the rising trills of orange-crowned warblers
yellow-rump's quick-witted whirs
Pacific Slope's *eeeeoooit!*
but today except for occasional winter wren bursts
it's silent

Fitting perhaps
silence lichen-drenched
allowing a chance to take it all in
this bumpy gelid finger-numbing ride
this steep slog up loose rock
every-which-way rain
ruts slicks big sticks old snow
where it looks and feels
like maybe March
no sign at all of gooseberry's
fuschia-starred tips
not even the leaves of *Trillium*…

Had to stop
near the top
push to a flattish spot
Hop on
Continue up

My guess?
In that pause
half in the clouds
half not
green shoots not yet dangling
bleeding hearts
in the late-spring mist
one persistent sperm
a hundred million confreres weakening
the egg's insistent lock
pushed like a coho
sniffing home
from a thousand miles

From here it hardly seems conceivable
not only the hostile environment
elevation makes
but the one I've made
twenty years internally
diaphragm & spermicide
dependable dauntless intruders
on any sperm or egg's design

Today's a first in fact
so I'm extra carefully tasting
when we reach the top
my husband's salty cheeks tongue lips
50 degrees warmer
than my hands
which hold his head
not forgetting to mention
we've beaten (again)
the odds...

Crown of Sonnets for a Son

1.

For this I've waited very long.
Waited, knowing little. And little did I know,
when first you settled in, I'd bleed. Didn't know
I'd crave Phad Thai, fish tacos, that strong-
willed, flat-tummied me as distant as dawn
just after sunset flashes green. You'd grow,
they said, from grain, to pea, to bean before I'd show,
but three weeks in I traded buttons for drawstrings.
I crawled, breast-stroked; you lapped at newly teeming lakes.
Twin pink hyacinths bloomed beside the fence; you sprouted lungs.
Praising your poppy-seed heart, your father rearranged the spice rack,
imagined you five, seasoning stream-caught trout. Headaches
did their best that spring to keep me dumb
but slowly I bungled toward instinct, making sense of facts.

2.

Slowly I bungled toward instinct, making sense of facts,
cuz really I needed both: to not just
accept, for instance, my baking bun was the size of a dust
mite, had a rudimentary spine, but that not a scrap
of will, not one neuron's worth of thought,
nothing, in short, I'd done (except to follow lust)
sprang to life. Slowly. Toward trust.
And as they split and split, so too our half-life of loss.
Before the trip to the store for the test,
before I peed in a cup (o so very positive),
my cheeks were vodka-rosy, Merlot-tinged.
Now when I spot a cardinal's crimson crest
or any speck of red, I rub my belly (*please live…*);
now, like Procyon to its aging twin, we're hinged.

3.

Now, like Procyon to its aging twin, we're hinged—
my mid-day almond snack your sustenance,
though soon enough you'll blurt *It's chance—*
parents shmarents…arbitrary! (Singeing

as I've singed). And when you roll your eyes at my orange
scarf, and when you want a certain pair of jeans
I'll venture back to this: a single, chirping finch, first green,
pump-handle call of a jay; I'll binge,
in other words, on memory stripped of fear,
on how I'll guess I used to live.
Then I'll shell out eighty bucks for Levis
you'll throw in a backyard pool and sear
with chlorine—white-speckled galaxies.
(Why is it I can't wait to hear you cry?)

4.

Why is it I can't wait to hear you cry
or coo, to say (distinctly) *ghee?* Pushing,
contractions, dilation, hospital's rush rush:
who needs it? (Me.) Week four I named you Ry;
each time I told a friend, imagined cramps.
Hid my growing womb, but gushed
to those who knew (*This week the spleen goes in!*). O luscious
naps: each afternoon I happily succumbed.
But when Stewart and Belle—our city's parent peregrines—
took turns knocking pigeons from the sky,
keeping their wobbly eyases warm, I swore
I'd never be *that* animal—that one-
tracked. Or understand their bobbing, beaky fear.
As for a higher—human—intelligence, I'm less sure.

5.

As for a higher—human—intelligence, I'm less sure,
especially here with your father, twenty feet above me
in a tree—face scrunched, forehead holding
a nest box firmly as he screws it in.
Never mind the snow like darting pins.
Never mind the temperature (six or seven, at best).
The kestrels, come May, will need a place to nest.
And though there's no guarantee they'll choose this tree,
I toss a bag of shavings he spreads on the floor
to lure them in. Not that we ever know
what or who will successfully breed—slow

sperm, unfused tubes, collapsing wombs, peril
of aging eggs. Today you weigh six potato chips;
I try to laugh at what I can't control.

6.

I try to laugh at what I can't control—
take hormonal ups and downs. One week I wept incessantly
at diaper ads, Stevie Wonder's "Isn't She Lovely?",
Peter Falk's old raincoat, road-kill squirrels.
Then (for no apparent reason), crawled up
like a hibernating mole, sobbing uncontrollably
till I remembered lunch with a friend. I grabbed my keys
and off I went—as if all of this were normal.
Later when I told your dad he seemed concerned.
Don't worry, I quipped, he doesn't grow ears till next week.
In truth, I worry more than laugh. Can't
fathom the news I'm not carrying a genetic mistake,
a vegetable, a something with holes in his heart.
You can lower the odds, but nothing's 100 percent.

7.

You can lower the odds, but nothing's 100 percent,
not snipping a piece of tissue surrounding this little prawn,
not amnio's endless needle, swearing off caffeine,
aspirin, alcohol. Adjust to paying rent
on a home you'll never own, to a screened-in
porch so riddled with moths you can't see in.
To cleanse their hearts and minds, the Lakota enter
a womb of mud they fill with steaming stones.
As the heat becomes unbearable they pray
to their mothers, focus on the pain of giving birth,
on the drum keeping time to an ancient song.
Will I learn to live with a fear that never leaves?
This floating fetus its own mysterious Earth.
For this I've waited very long.

Getting Kicked by a Fetus

Like right before you reach your floor, just
before the door of an elevator opens.
Like the almost imperceptible
springs you waded through
in Iroquois Lake.
Carbonation.
Twitch.

Sometimes high and jabby near the ribs;
sometimes low and fizzy like a pie
releasing steam, like beans
on the stovetop—slow
simmer,

like the shimmer of incoming tide—hot, soft sand
meeting waves, slosh bringing sand crabs
that wriggle invisibly in.

And sometimes a school of herring
pushing through surf,
or a single herring

caught from a pier like a sliver of moon rising in the west;
sometimes a tadpole stuck in a pond growing smaller
and smaller, a puddle of mud, squirmy like worms—
now your left, now your right. Sometimes

neon flickering, like that Texaco sign near Riddle, Oregon—
from a distance it read TACO, but up close
the faintest glow, an occasional E or X,
like an ember re-igniting.

Like seeing your heartbeat through the thinnest part
of your foot, sunken well between ankle and heel,
reminder of a world beneath your skin, world
of which you know little,

and the pond growing smaller and smaller, soon the rolling waves
like the ones you dove into at Bradley Beach, at Barneget,
growing less frequent, your giant ocean
drying up, your little swimmer

sinking, giving way
to the waves
of his birth.

After Drinking the Orange Liquid for the Glucose Tolerance Test

I take a seat by the window near a table strewn
with *House Beautiful, Metropolitan Home*, think of all the others—

moms to be, the genetically fated, those with the unlucky predilection
for making too much insulin—Emily's debauches of dew.

Of all those in love with sweetness—fathers raising flutes
to perfectly shaven cheeks, to cream satin trains of unfathomable lengths,

of the bright red water I poured each morning into a plastic feeder
for the single hummingbird who arrived each dusk

like the first cool breeze in months. One or two sips
and off she'd go to who knows where—a neighbor's

blooming saguaro, an even sweeter brew
neither I nor anyone else could duplicate.

Like this moment here in this room—
gurgle of fish tank, page of a magazine turning,

the receptionist's "I don't know where she is, to tell you the truth."

Picking a Name While Picking Blackberries

for Riley Francesco Cook

Now that we haven't named you
Beauregard, Bickford, or Beryl, not a field

of heather, not golden or peaceful, not
the all-wise, exalted one; now that we've passed up

"dweller at the oaks," "people of a different speech,"
"from the cottage on the winding path," we settle slowly

into all your twenty-six weeks, wonder what you think
of daylight, caponata, jerk of laughter, tears.

Now that we've disregarded "ford at the peak,"
"dove keeper," "mortal man," we think of places

we'll take you—Umbria and Oscaloosa, Chang Mai
and Cheney—to what birds we'll hoist you above

our own astonished heads, to what waves you'll see,
as we've seen, the snouts of sea lions, seaweed like lace.

Now that we've found your one true name,
not "from the deer's spring," "famous wolf," "maker

of tile or bricks," I ask your father to help me reach
the farthest, prickliest branch—most precious berry yet.

What They Don't Tell You About the Ninth Month

is about your fingers how they tingle go numb ache
like your 88-year old grandmothers
who spent her whole life knitting or kneading

forty years rolling cigars in a Kingston factory
the one who wears a cast because she didn't feel like waiting
for her daughter to help her down the stairs

after four o'clock mass *I put it on ice…it don't hurt too bad*
so you raise them in the air it's 3:37 a.m. ten twenty thirty time
you waken who's counting your own half-snore half-gasp

a dying dinosaur at the end of the dying Cretaceous
and in between you're dreaming 8th Avenue's a river
buildings shaped by the mud of a deluge

by the great surge of the Hudson
but it's the present and you're sharing the view
with a childhood friend twenty stories above

isn't it something? men scrambling to stop it
clean it up wash the mud from the brick no use
waves engulfing glass marble chrome all the little gadgets

Dopplers and stethoscopes the comfort of pillows
the cleanliness of rubber gloves of gowns
this mud your guttural groans your opening womb

fury of all-but-forgotten blood

III.

*I Don't Know What I Want, Only that
I'm Desperate for It*

Song for a Newborn

Oh my Double Thick Pork Chop,
my Prawn Tequila-kissed,
Most Pico of Pico de Gallos:
bless your brain—
its fluids & aqueducts, its ventricles,
the little fountains splashing.
Bless your arms which hang,
outstretched, in sleep,
as if conducting an orchestra,
a tune I'll never know.
Bless your capillaries
like the roots of Early Girls,
your large intestine like dozens
of miniature knackwursts.
Bless your liver, its 500 functions.
Bless your sternum, your scapula—
heck: bless all your 206 bones.
Someday you'll understand the humor
of an opening refrigerator eliciting
the Pope's voice, the irony of a logging saw
painted with grizzly bears, towering conifers,
a bright blue river, but for now I'll have to settle,
my Sugar-Cane Showered Scallop, my Swimming Angel,
for your smile which says Braised Chicken,
Cilantro Dumplings, Romaine's Most Tender Hearts.

Gravitas

A quarter cow in a cardboard box
is heavy can barely be lifted

the cow had eyes had legs
the cow now only its roasts

I carry it from trunk to house
ground round and chuck

up the stairs and into the freezer
discover my chore is not only

burden but cheerless
there is much in a marriage

that is cheerless the husband wanting
a windy wisp-ness web-like escarolian

though not exactly the opposite
of pot roast which is clotted leaves a trail

they made a son a deep-mouthed glint
crocus mud-specked oak if

there is sky if there is grieving
the meat which is flank

which is rump or rib not the aimless
aspen's swirl not the bed

which is heavy on her frothy thoughts
on her flimsy foolish head

Crazy

as in J-bird, loon, loony tunes. Loonier
than you'll ever be, especially

if you never have a kid. (Even if you do).
One in a thousand you'll end up like me,

certain you've been shot, killed, sent through the long, slow
stove of cremation, your not-there dad in the hallway, your newborn's

face in the peeling plaster of your loony bin room,
and of course it won't happen you'll greet,

when you take a leak beneath the fire alarm, the devil's grin,
or in the sloping, slender handles of your bathroom sink,

a sloping, slender saint. Not likely your mother
will fly 3,000 miles to find you unable to see

let alone speak, or, if speaking, loudly, of the universe
as a giant, glowing bowel. Less so you'll unhinge,

lose a screw, your marbles, go bananas or ape,
become the fruitcake of endless re-gifting, believe

you've the power to stop the Unabomber, send your loved ones
to hell. *Where ya going? Crazy. Wanna come?* As if asking

enough could make it so—*as in if this were a play…*
though, in truth, it was no kind of book you'd want to read,

with no kind way to return you to your rocker, re-stitch,
depixelate, unmadden your March-hared, over-

Niagara-without-the-barrel brain. Gone mad, you'd say, secure,
as I was once secure, in your witted, ungripped head, believing

we never return, never stop trying to jump from windows,
a little closer to the god who tells us he needs a break,

could we please, for a while, take over? As if always
nobody's home. Raving. Stark. As if that could explain

flying over Seattle with the wicked witch. Forty minutes
without blinking. As if by joking, calling it cuckoo, gaga,

wacky, or bonkers, we could inoculate ourselves
from the batty and the beany. As if no one—least of all me,

least of all you—ever returns from the uppermost story,
ever stops rounding the minus-a-few-buttons bend.

At the Sayres Park Rowing and Sailing Center, Lake Washington, Seattle

This is the body of water I once considered
slipping into—step, step, another step—

till like Virginia Woolf in a black and billowy
bathing suit, the air would seep as it does

from a loosely tied balloon. This is the crow
which represents the crowing I'd wake to—

crowing without the crow. These are the gulls
that preened, pecked, molted to brilliant white

all without my notice. This is the body of water
I planned, like the bread that ducks can't always catch,

to sink into. And this is the brightly tuxedoed bufflehead
who, over and over, dives under, disappears, pops back up.

Harborview

By the roots of my hair some god got hold of me
—Sylvia Plath

By the roots of my hair, by the reinforced elastic
of my floral Bravado bra, by the fraying strands

of my blue-checked briefs, some god's gotten hold of me,
some god's squeezed hard the spit-up rag of my soul, rung me

like the little girl who rang our doorbell on Halloween, took
our M&Ms *is your baby okay? Why did they take him away?*

Some god's got me thinking my milk's poison, unfit
for a hungry child, some god's got me pacing,

set me flying like the black felt bats dangling
in the hall, some god so that now I can't trust my best friend's

healing hands, the Phad Thai she's spooning beside the rice(ditto
to the meds the doctors say will help me sleep) *Poison poison!*

as if the god who's got hold of me doesn't want me
well, doesn't want my rapid-fire brain to slow,

wants this ride for as long as it lasts, wants to take it
to its over-Niagara-in-a-barrel end, which is where

this god is taking me, one rung at a time, one ambulance,
one EMT strapping me in, throwing me off this earth,

cuz I've not only killed my son but a heap of others too.
Some god's got me by my shiny golden locks, by my milk-

leaking breasts, got me in this hospital, wisps like white scarves
circling my head, wisps the voices of men *back to bed you whore!*

Some god till I'm believing I've been shot, guts dribbling out,
till I'm sure I've ridden all over town in a spaceship, sure

I'm dead, a ghost, a smoldering corpse, though not before I'm holding up
a shaking wall, urging the others to help me (a plane about to land

on our heads), though soon enough thrown down by two night nurses,
strapped to a bed, though for weeks the flowers my in-laws sent

charred at the tips (having been to hell and back), clang of pots,
hissing shower, the two blue pills my roommate left in the sink,

all signals of doom, though some god got hold of me,
shook and shook me long and hard, she also brought me back.

Explaining Current Events to a One-Year Old

The sky will never be this gray—belly of a mallard,
body of a plane emerging from clouds—
layer upon layer in every direction.

Gone are the goldfinches, barn swallows, violet greens.
Welcome the juncos, their metronome calls,
welcome the play of light and dark,

the occasional patch of blue, the ever-present wind.
The dogwood's aflame. The big leaf maple's
right behind her. Lots of things

could easily ignite, which is why we dress you
in flame retardant pajamas, circle your neck
with light-blue hearts.

The larkspur we waited for all summer
is finally blooming, but it's wrong—
bent beneath a cedar, snaking up,

snaking right back down. When your eyes are closed,
I focus on your eyelids. Your eyelids
and your breath, breath of the wind,

the cottonwood's applause. Because you open like a flower,
I leave a light on in the hall. Because each day
the red in the leaves a little redder,

I wish they were more like lullabies of unknown origin—
like the one you wake from to cake and pretty horses.
To explain them, I need to explain

country, God, passion, loyalty, love.
Because I don't know how else
to begin, I begin with love.

Four a.m.

Why is it the things you never think about at four in the afternoon
consume you at 4 a.m.? For instance why am I lying here just after
    the newspaper
bangs the front door asking myself how did I throw away all
    those letters
my mother's been sending

since college the ones telling me *sun's streaming temp near 40 may*
    snow
letters in which always a pot of soup is simmering *time to use up*
old vegetables hundreds of recipes Better than Ketchup

Acorn Squash Chili Tofu Sticks in long hand
with side notes *(cut sugar in half or substitute with cane juice)*
letters catching me up with family news *Uncle Willy's at a baseball*
    conference

in Pensacola Carol Anne's expecting her fourth Lottie's touring the West
letters *remind me to tell you the one about the cantaloupe*
the potential wife needing to know the square root

of minus one (dad told it better than me) letters
I might've easily stuffed in bags *wife & kids left him*
at the peak of tree cutting season told her she had two choices:

a parachute or a raft letters which did pile up
was it in my twenties? *Winston Sloan*
put in a new lawn! Even though

I was moving around a lot but then
I must've forgotten *how about some unshelled nuts*
a see-through unbreakable container how much I'd need her

gotta go brush teeth run out to look at a house just an idea driveway too steep
asking 159,000 forgot I'd ever be a mother my son
at four a.m. *mama? mama?* The letters I'll write him.

My Son Asks 'What's a Torrent?'

It's a womb, a swarm of worms, a swirling, untamed horn.
It's our bobbing, bubbling future, the dry leaf careening
beneath its branch as the first fat raindrops fall.

It's a gushing, surging, riffling, swiftness; it's here,
where the river turns; there, where we heard the dipper
like water singing;

and now it's splashing, banging banks, swishing
past an overhanging willow like a girl with a comb
pulling and pulling her tangled hair.

Whole trees (it can happen; it happens) unleashing.
It's a swelling and bulging: the Skagit, the Sauk,
the Snoqualmie, the Stillaguamish. What the fishermen call

off color, an every-which-wayness all utterance (short
on restraint, hard to decipher), a violence purely, refreshingly
amoral, as in *Now I'll go this way, not that way,* cabins and coffins

loosening from comfortable clay. The mystery of mud stains
on three story houses. Bursting, confusing, it could be
carrying your books, your wallet, your living room sofa;

it's friction's slurry and spin, the whole big, dark tugging and gurgling
jostle and sway of everything liquid, our roiling,
rapid-riding brains.

What a Piece of Work is a Man

has already of course been said and besides
even Shakespeare didn't believe it
following it as he did with all that

quintessence of dust which is maybe
why I'm reminded as I watch a giraffe
lift its outstretched neck past vertical

its nine inch tongue inching nine inches closer
to a clump of leaves it can't quite reach
of that Sistine Chapel hand

how at the last unlike a God the paragon instead
of the almost reaching of the oh so close
of all day my son

Mama there's a cherry on that floor Mama look at that balloon
forcing me to observe single things meant-to-be
symbols of freedom and love

cast about or caught in trees at singularity at single –hood or –dom
at not with the man not this morning noble in reason not
when he showed me with his hands how close he was

to moving out *Mama* (when he sees I can't swing him between me
and nothing) *we need Da-da we need him right now*

His Favorite Color is Green

All shades all permutations
of say the shiny glabrous stem
of a shooting-out-from-winter daffodil
of Astroturf like just-before-blooming phlox

the long-&-narrow-little-or-large-town street sign
the big square Missoula Sioux City Throgsneck Bridge
along the freeway with horsetail astragalus vetch

the Libyan flag whipping over one point oh
three percent arable land
shimmer of mallard's head

or lighter...the under-ripe fruit
he does his best to enjoy
olivaceousness of kinglets
mama calliope warming her eggs
those clusters that fall in April or May
from Norway maples onto sidewalks
we stroller past
custard of scooped out avocado

or dark as say its skin... seaweed hemlock
dinosaur kale...picnic tables of city parks

The vegetables he hates
The garbage trucks he loves

The semi-spicate the glume-ful the spikelike the membranous
The shallowly bifid the twisted the sticky the hollow
The most common & palatable known
from near Corvallis from near Boise
Whorlwort Beckmannia False Brome

His world's frondy
Maidenhair gone haywire
His world's licorice wet (also deer & lady)
His world's hickory buckeye slippery elm

I kneel to find him something emerald
something emerald & squiggly

I hardly knew him that first spring he fit in a playground swing
ratcheting a metal bar along a chain
down & down till it fit

So much of his world so much of this world
even where plowed where fires even in cities
a hispid persistence

I wanted him to come along but he wouldn't
I wanted him to hurry
I needed to tell him what Horace said
about the goddess Envy
("leave no offerings")

Piles of clippings giant piles of invasive ivy
the neighbor's ghost-shaped shrubs harmless giants
while he sings his crocodile song

While He Naps

Like tulips wrapped in cellophane, a nap is a beautiful thing.
Like the wind before it starts to rain, a nap is beautiful
like a lawn near a lake where you lay yourself down,

remove from a knapsack crackers and brie
while out on the water a red-breasted merganser,
while up in the woods a hairy woodpecker's peek!

Half an hour, an hour tops. Time enough to watch a flock
of chickadees glean invisible insects, time enough
to write a letter, enjoy, alone, a portabello sandwich.

If silence is golden it's the gold of the sunset
you missed folding laundry, sunset over rooftops,
of bread from overripe bananas, of glowworms, the gold of stars

you'd never seen—Southern Cross and Magellanic Clouds
replacing dippers and sisters. But the letter goes
into a drawer half written. But in remembering

the bottle you forget the binoculars. But you don't know the date
let alone the name of the hut where after seeing those glittery worms
you claimed a bunk and called it a night. Every minute

till he wakes—stuffed animals idle, rattle still, nothing
but the occasional boat engine, passing conversation, the steady lap
of waves—a miracle. Holding him on your hip while washing lettuce,

stick what's left of the macaroni and cheese into the fridge
a distant memory, sound of his cries as foreign as gulls
on a wide New Zealand beach.

I Don't Know What I Want, Only that I'm Desperate for it

—Kim Addonizio

I want the piece of lime green yarn my son strung up
with butterflies and stars, the care he took to ask

Mama, do you like white? Is blue your favorite color?
though not the face he made when I had to remove a few—

pale yellow, metallic pink—to attach the string to just above
my foot (may the yarn never give; may the beads not stray

to unfathomable depths). And I want the purple chrysanthemums
to stay purple, the ever-pitter of flying grasshopper, crest and sheen

of Steller's Jay, even its penchant for stealing grapes,
though not its blood, its nervous flaps, its back and forth

from fence to ground, that fluttering, flickering tail.
Chrysanthemums, and the sunflowers, too, of course,

their heads heavily eastward, heavily sexy, with sexual parts,
their proliferation of seeds a dead ringer (the bees

utterly fraught). And I want my hair messy
like their hair, the past-due raggedness of rays, for once,

an asset. I want, like my son, the milk when the milk's
in my hand, mama when mama's beside him, willing

his aching to stop. And I want this shimmery shift dress
always to shimmer, don't want the hummingbirds

to go, though we're down to one, the occasional buzz
that was once cacaphonic (with metronomic ticking).

And I want to be famous, not like pinecones at the end
of a branch, or socks curled up in a young woman's shoes

but a fame like yo-yos, Kleenex, the Northern Spye.
I don't know what I want, but I like the days

that aren't as hot as they could be, sway
of construction paper dinosaurs we hung from the ceiling:

Don't take those.

Tit for Tat

If socks matched, if perfect teeth, there goes knack
for whipping up, at six am, Cowboy Coffee Cake.

If could sing, with perfect pitch "Three Blind Mice,"
might unwieldily whack, do much worse.

If picking up clothes from drycleaners, waving
white and red slip, good-bye infectious laugh.

If fresh breath, if 20/20, if tires never treaded
stripe-y white, bon voyage excitement

for Struthiomimus's sprint. If not one patch stubble,
no interest in dawn; if no dilly-dally, no dawdle

at Lottie Mott's, no thrill when son exclaims,
on windy afternoon, "I bet those leaves have wings!"

If watch band fixed, not swirling in second rinse,
gone the playground—lying back, slinging legs

on cool, cool slide; if no lost keys, lost phone, lost lists,
no sifting gravel through all ten fingers, breathing in the sun.

What Do You Do When You're Blue?

I look up at the sky, go "Me, too!"
Not because I thoroughly understand

about waves—their length and speed—
the way they bounce off bits of air,

creating, for instance, the color of day,
not because I understand the eye,

how it, too, plays a part in helping us see
a certain-colored sky, excited receptors

equaling cerulean, though in this park,
thanks to smog, a little lighter than light.

When I'm blue I open the paper, go straight
to the *Science Times*, to those for whom

the day's all anticipation, the long wait
for the fade to black, to lift the lens cap,

hunker down on what's above, on orbs
perhaps supporting life. I'm uplifted,

I'll admit, by the notion of peering,
ever hopeful, toward a darkening sky.

I take a long, long walk, thanking
with each step my lucky stars

(by the light of the moon, by the specks
of unknown suns, I'm alive).

IV.

*Forgetfulness the Great Bronchial Tree from
Which I'm Swinging*

Forgetfulness the Great Bronchial Tree from Which I'm Swinging

Forgetfulness the great bronchial tree from which I'm swinging
    nimble as a baby gorilla clenched fists slipping
through the farthest branch
    forgetfulness engaging my trapezius
reaching for what's inside my I thought safely guarded
    box of bones where I can't retrieve the word
for the thing in which I'm soaking
    forgetfulness falling to the back of the throat
back there with the uvula with the fauces
    not exactly the tip of the tongue more like the sublingual duct
my keys in the yard with the soupy tomatoes
    with the weepy zucchini
over the fence pecking seed
    forgetfulness the great Volkmann's canal
from which each day I hop a water taxi
    that deep and bony dentin
though forgetfulness too in the ever-eroding
    enamel the interstitial spaces my thoughts deciduous
teeth all eruption and loss oh these ossified
    ossifications my husband's groaning
you forget everything epiglottis glotted
    fed-up-ness swelling his Adam's apple
proof of insurance recipe for *ouefs a la neige*
    a Ho Jo's in Far Rockaway
which keeps on calling
    claims I spent the night
aqueous fluids rushing the scene *Impossible!*
    my vitreous body holding firmly giving light
it's just I'm not sure I paid the mortgage
    plexus of *meant to should've not again!* Limbic system
lesioned? just the woman on the other end
    says here you checked in 9/19

Cabbage

Cruciferae from crucifix
this purple epistolary
this white crustacean
running down the middle
this spider in a web
my son keeps asking
to lift him up to see
show me that web
though when I do
it's gone crawled off
but this one's still
and always not
to somewhere else
it is something like wine
a merlot a burgundy
it is something like
a bruise beneath
the eye vulnerable
capillaries at the back
of the knee it didn't exactly
yield but had to be split
with a cleaver I'm not sure
I'm the intended reader
also something of a blush
a beet-like remembering
also the ragged edge
of unfurling leaf

Low Tide Walk with Mary Grace

Even when it was low the water so far out it seemed it would never
Mary Grace her gum boots beige pants *high tide!* and we all ran
toward the road then *low tide!* and we all ran toward

the like I said impossibly far and the red sea nettle
don't touch though I doubt it was even alive
more about the not-moving-or-poking

concept though not exactly explicitly stated on principle
like the guy who carried the crab fifty yards from its home
by the big barnacled rock *take it back exactly*

which I'm not sure he regretted but as he carefully
Mary Grace looking on I was teaching my son
how to loosen rocks from sand the scrambling

and squirting the splashing not discouraging quite enough
the need to hold to keep to hurt my allegiance
to women like Mary Grace to the barnacle-

munching whelks the prehistoric isopods this frenzy of feeding
that comes and goes that came and went where now
these rocks and pools this warm green lace

Till We Found Ourselves Thinking

if he wants to pee down that attic vent arcing to where
the good clothes sleep the little jagged sequins
flowers orange and fuchsia spaghetti straps

straight down to where the safest way out
is still in our nighties and slippers where all our best hunches
the one where even after T. rex swears he'll lose

his flesh-ripping teeth Edmontonia struts
his bony plates the one about the brightest stars needing
their ever so faint companions to hold them firmly

in place refuse to coalesce…so be it so be it
we can always send the furnace to the cleaners infuse
the wooden slats with lavender vanilla pillow mist

promotes tranquility fire up the weed whacker sip lemonade
as we ogle Air Force One the 87 telephones the surgery bay
with pull out operating table we can always dream

of taking a shower right there in the nose rivulets and spray
as we look out on the contours of canyons on rivers stretching
to places where no one says *ruthless killing of American citizens*

and others the sleeping berth for two maybe a demon's
in charge though we can't as Jack London said wait for inspiration
we have to go after it with a club to stay aloft indefinitely

a conference with video fax computer really any
plane carrying the president even without refueling
which it does midair

till we found ourselves thinking if we can maybe
he could admit that is the errors of his ways
but what it must be like to float from room to room

unafraid from a treadmill reading signs without a translator
and after weeks in the field which is actually our 1916 Craftsman
we can't tell exactly where the smell is coming from

though it's been pointed out the shiny silver pipe
in our own closet's gunked with sticky yellow
might be once we break through these clouds fold

our cards swivel a couple more times these leather seats
we might find it in ourselves though it might take patience
might mean talking to aim it in the place where it belongs

Suite for the Visiting Dead

It's the Day of the Dead. It's the day, if you're willing, to don
your sombrero, to step courageously into your green tamale
shoes, into your most unpoker posole face, if you allow yourself,

to sink deeply into your jalapeño heart, to believe
the ones you've loved and lost are with you,
having awakened, at death, from a dream;

it's a day, if your mother loved cabbage, to fix her
a steaming plate of *halushki,* the green head shredded fine,
sautéed in butter, dusted with pepper and salt,

to remember how she loved the polka. Also kielbasa, pork roast,
spaghetti, singing in Polish, also the occasional swig of Bud,
percolated coffee, chicken soup. If someone who's dead

ever got your goat, tell it again. Laugh
because you were had, were made a fool.
Laugh, and the not so dead will laugh with you,

because today the line between them and us
is porous as a sopapilla, breathes the living air
through tiny holes. Because the woman who sold you

meringue powder for your sugar skulls
told you her people keep right on doing what they did in life—
"barber, baker, prostitute…" rest assured:

Lieutenant Artimus D. Brassfield, who wrote home
"I don't know what we're doing here," though he might
have died while fixing a tank, mostly he's shooting hoops.

And Emmie Teal, who wants only to crack the box open enough
to hold, one last time, her son's hand, can hold her son's hand,
can dance, today, with her son, the funky chicken and the bump.

And Sergeant Audrey Bell, who grew up on his mother's ketchup
and mayonnaise sandwiches, can keep on eating; and you,
who looked up from your pharmacology textbook

to the men in green on your porch, your husband's come down today
from the 13th level, the one reserved for soldiers, for mothers who died
in childbirth, he's down here digging ditches

for his toy soldiers, here with my grandmother as she rolls the dough
for her famous nut rolls, counts her 167th perogie before
she slips them, one by one, into a cast iron pot,

as my uncle, smoking a late afternoon stogy, admires his roses,
my aunt as she bends to gather windfall plums,
my son running right through them—

"Come find me! I'm hiding!" (believing,
because he can't see us, we can't see him),
running right through Sergeant Paul Johnson,

who takes a diving leap for the star-studded sky, passes,
on his way to Delphinus, Private Rachel Bosveld
as she picks up her brush, puts the finishing strokes

on a row of Torrey pines. Yes, there's traffic;
the streets are crowded; the market is bustling.
We're on our way, as the threads of darkness descend,

to olives, cheeses, the best garbanzos,
to the mangled strewn like yesterday's pumpkins
(Do they pray for us? Do we pray for them?).

As Rumi says, "I was dead, then alive, /
weeping, then laughing"; "I am a sky where the spirits live."
For we do not lie down easily. For the dawn is thick with bodies,

living and dead.

My Son Considers the Mockingbird

and death
whether people still have birthdays
when they're dead

my son considers the mockingbird
in the song I sing to soothe him

but when I sing
you'll still be the sweetest little baby in town

but that mockingbird didn't sing but when
I reassure him *but that diamond ring wouldn't shine*

nose stuffed with woe head heavy with defective billy goat
this son of mine who asks *do I get to come back*

as a puffin? Will you be a puffin too?
this son of mine who knows

the dog named Rover won't bark
that the horse and cart will fall like the cradle

he tells me he'll always be there to catch
the baby having nothing

nothing but the burden of his ever-outstretched arms

To a Giant Allium

I'm thinking beauty parlor
a seventy-something stuck beneath

a dryer's desiccating wind
I'm thinking swim cap

from my mother's mother's time
hat atop the wig she wore

after her hair started thinning
what we thought only a man

could lose and lose
hat with those hyacinth-colored blooms

you could buy if you never ever
wanted what you held

in a vase to droop
and of course I'm thinking

4th of July that time we walked
the lawns of Squibb and Modess

to reach an even bigger field
lay back on our quilt to watch

a little part of the sky once in a while
explode like a lavender Hostess sno-ball

I have a pair of earrings
clip-ons tight bunches six-petaled

and just like this I'm down to one
the florettes I think they're florettes

tightly bunched there must be hundreds
if two heads are better how much better

six hundred fifty seven? Some stand out
a little farther I hate to say it

but like a Grandma
hat and wig those crazy floral prints

like gawking heads from a crowded train
though no train ever quite this purplish

none so completely arrayed

Poem in French

After Paul Hoover

I have one son and two wishes.
One is the kind you blow out.

I have one bad dream,
two cups for my morning tea.

Once I sat on a beach, the Siuslaw
slamming the Pacific, twice I rode

a silent, silent boat. I had never before
been two people: my outbursts, my longings,

his train pulling away: *A bientot!*
I have two thoughts and one of them is ugly.

At night I'm a thorn in your thorny side,
two feathers sticking sideways

from a hummingbird's glowing gorget.

What in the World Were You Thinking?

Before we even know you're there, you've taken
your little jaunt, splitting as you go, settling cozily in.

Just a mass of cells—thin-walled, hollow, just a blastocyst
growing like any seed (though I'm thinking pumpkin, salt

on your father's tongue); two-layererd, with your yolk sac
open, a private aquarium where you'll do your lapping.

A yolk-less yolk sac, in fact, meso and endo, all this
and gastrulation, which we somehow missed

that hottest week, our cooler down by the river.
And now there's a primitive streak in the center

of the upper layer. And now there's a notochord
and something pinching: your own digestive tract!

Soon you'll be sporting a tail and gills; in a few days
webbed fingers, my little fry, my ducky prawn.

Before we know it you'll be half brain, the sudden
budding of eyes. *Rapid differentiation*, the textbook says,

which I take to mean eat all your vegetables—
the crooked carrots, potatoes in their jackets, even

the stinging mustard. Which I take to mean go ahead
and dig up the blossoming thistle, but give in, give in

to lying down. Littlest one, just in case you were wondering,
you weren't exactly planned, but neither were the marigolds

that blanket half our garden. All you need to be human will shortly arrive.

The Forbidden Fruit

was probably an apricot
but is almost always depicted

as shiny and red, the tree
the barren woman's supposed

to roll around beneath,
wash her hands with its juice.

How like us to choose,
for our eye-opening snack,

the one that hybridizes
with any other Malus, so that

planting a seed from a small and sour
might well yield a large and sweet.

"A good year for apples,
a good year for twins,"

The Dictionary of Superstitions said,
though weren't we glad when it turned out

not to be true. At the turn of the century,
Tobias Miller brought to Gold Hill, Oregon,

the King, the Northern Spy, the Yellow Transparent,
the Gravenstein, and the Greening,

though we're not sure what we're gathering—
stripey reds we peel and core for sauce,

yellows blushing in the summer sun.
When they ate of it, it tasted good,

twice as good, as say, eternity,
which could not be folded into cake,

which could not be put up or pressed.

Amanita calyptrata

The way we enter this world—an egg, a growing stalk,
a body sheathed in cottony-white. The way we, too, emerge—

swathed in waxy vernix, sometimes still partially cloaked
in our amniotic sac, our sturdy homes like this universal veil,

not quite ready to let us go. This was what I was thinking
the first time I spotted, in the rapidly dampening woods,

Amanita calyptrata, the fall rains forging a river down our dusty drive.
Mushrooms Demystified likened them to *rare and secretive birds, a sunrise forming,*

a blanket of clouds, but to me they seemed oddly familiar, not unlike
what went on in millions of female bodies, not unlike what had happened

more than once in the womb of this 92-year old now pointing to the picture,
asking me to confirm the dull-orange cap, cream-colored gills, fishy scent.

And who would have the nerve to doubt her, this woman who told me
over a meal of her own Chinook of her early attempts at landing fish

at the mouths of these local creeks, back in the 30s? So, tonight I'm eating
Amanita, for how can I, how could anyone, pipe up with a *sorry I'm passing?*

Like passing up, despite the risks, the chance to raft this raging Rogue,
like turning tail, for no good reason, on your own expanding

womb, though you have to admit you're not quite up for an icy dousing,
though the memory of the group who mistook a related bunch

for straw mushrooms, not *phalloides*, remains especially sharp.
In the end all your confidence will amount to less, much less,

than this pile of caps and stalks beside the sink—sleeplessness,
anxiety, estrogen's rapid decline—but off you go on your own raft,

Clonazipam and a baby nurse your two sworn antidotes. Off you go
to face whatever upset, whatever peril, this blessed bounty brings.

V.

My Body Will Run With the Weeds Some Day

Poem Ending with a Snippet from an Old Familiar Song

The guy who makes my latte says I'll be giving birth
in a week or less even sooner if I take
a good long walk

when I tell him no—more like four to six
he shoots me a face like bitter coffee
oh no I'm sure of it a week

The Russian ladies at Frenchy's Salon say seven months is fine
but not eight—eight's not a good number (superstition
unique to the Cossacks? The Ukraine?

The far reaches of Georgia?) Speaking of reaches
my unborn daughter bears down
on my deepest nether region

bears and bears beyond my own antipodes
excavates with her fists my uterus
bushwhacks my furriest forest

head pressing so hard on my pubic bone
that when I wake to pee my privates
pinched and puckered small

and insignificant hardly there compared to her big wide brain
o my little cupcake swirls of pink icing surrounding
your jolting and tossing I know I won't carry you

forever won't always feel that foot but little good
when I'm struggling to find a comfy spot
on the couch sidelined to keep

my vena cava from straining little good as I waddle again
toward a glass of water my girl inside me spelunking
a tisket a tasket a green and yellow basket...

Once in a Blue Moon

we say, not looking to see if the moon's done its thing
twice in a single month, if it's gone full-circle, fat

and happy, thinned to an infant's fingernail, then waxed back
round and full a second time, the whole shebang crammed

into twenty-eight nights, not looking quite closely enough
at the calendar, at that night of moonlessness mid-month,

when the Milky Way hung from our sky like a giant beach towel
from a backyard clothesline, no light to stifle the stars,

at the night, give or take a few, we made you,
though more correct to say the night made us, nothing

more pressing than a male moth's need to track for a mile
the scent of a mate. And watching it rise each dusk

a little fatter, a little happier, a comfort, a privilege,
a little secret expanding, eliciting light.

Lately I'm Capable Only of Small Things

—Olena K. Davis

like hanging a pair of panties on the line,
whisking eggs into oil, slowly adding the flour.

Lately, it's a pretty big deal going out on a limb—
adding a little cocoa to the usual mix. Lately I'm wanting

silence, but in truth an occasional cricket's chirp
is okay, too. I've noticed, of late, how my son,

like me, sees pictures in the floorboards—mosquitoes
and moths, the faces of friends, though unlike him

I've been needing to tell someone about the bright blue wings
of a jay as it disappeared in a clump of darkening green.

Usually I wouldn't think of it, but then I saw
a spider like a tiny crab curled up on our beige duvet.

Also, noises from the kitchen (had a squirrel broken in?).
And though the light is far from fading, soon, if I want,

I can listen to the news on the crank-up radio, to what the Dow,
today, has done. Lately, I'm surprised how the trees keep themselves

from falling, how mostly stable this sloping, unpredictable earth.

By the 6th Month

I'd forgotten what it was
to be a body not being kicked

by another
not to be carrying

not only my own
(as the ultrasound technician

said) still plentiful eggs
but my daughter's too (eggs

of a granddaughter or grandson)
the same way in the 60s

my mother carried
what would be my son

More than sitting
on any board on having a say

in some foundation's future
it was a place of extreme privilege

great esteem
though at the same time rarely spoken of

crowded out by discussions of how to roll out crust
whether to ice the cake or leave it

Begging to Differ

You had no choice but to ...join our joy, to dance
into my belly and rest / untroubled for 9 lovely months ...
—Laurie Albanese, *Our Bundle of Joy*

Fat, fucking hooey. Big, fat hunk of hulking, honking.
Hefty up heaved hunk right from those first aversions

to coffee, tomatoes, couscous, feta, anything served
more than once. Joining our joy? I might, just might, buy that—

joy of the day we conceived, or at least I think we conceived,
then hiked to Kelsey Creek where we watched

salmon pool up just below jagged boulders.
Skittish. Skid addling as we approached.

So unlike the sperm surrounding the egg,
breaking down the barriers that would soon

become our so-called dancing girl. But first bring on
the nosebleeds and the heartburn, the migraines

requiring codeine, bring on the nausea, that 6-month
stiff neck, waiting for results from the 2-in-100-causes-

miscarriage Chorionic Villous Sampling. Bring on the ultra-
sensitive ultrasounds (to screen out missing fingers, toes),

bring on the little dotted lines like vectors sashaying
along the screen, the carefully measured kidneys, lungs, tibias,

heart. Hooey altogether to lovely, our joy by now
the size of a no-see-um, opposite of joy

as I'm cocooned inside plastic for an MRI
(*we need to rule out aneurysm*). Hooey to any

would-be mom who says a fetus rests—
mine jolted me from sleep, bore down

till I puked—puked up not only juice
and crackers but water, plain water.

She didn't dance; she galloped. She didn't
do-see-do, hokey-pokey, or hullabaloo;

unhaltingly, she hammered; didn't divide
but devoured. The cosmos dances,

but an embryo? I see her more
as taking up shop, blow torch in one hand,

jack hammer in the other. Constantly flailing
two feisty fists. Making much more

than whirlpools in her mini-Jacuzzi.
It wasn't my womb to begin with.

Surely, those nine-some months, it was hers
and hers alone, till she got too big

to make her turns, to run her rumbling rudders,
till it was time for her to make her raucous, ruby-red debut.

I Can't Write

about her birth—about the way, when finally, after an eternity
of curling in and screaming, they plopped her on my chest

like a hot, wet seal, like something straight out of a warm
long-ago ocean, something slippery and covered with fur—

but I can write about the clock and its second hand,
how I gauged my progress by its slow and gentle circling

while I bounced on a blue ball, brought my cervix inch by inch
to ten. But I can't write, exactly, about dilation—how I stayed at three

till long past twelve, how progression didn't really begin
till after the almost-full moon had risen high enough to view it,

if we'd wanted, from that 5th floor brimming, overbrimming, with moaning
or pacing, passing again and again that giant yellow and red mangle

of a Deborah Butterfield horse, where instead we occupied ourselves
with ice water, heat packs, string cheese, spray from a Jacuzzi's jets—

or the number of times I pushed, but I can tell you that later that morning,
from three mini-blinded windows, I could hear the voices of children,

of mothers telling them to settle down, how I wished my womb, like theirs
(I presumed) had returned to the size of a fist. And I can tell you about

my bed, how I could lower it, how I could make it rise like a chair,
a ready-made chair for nursing, how in that bed I wished my daughter

were older than half a day, where both of us smelled not only of yeast
but of the acrid, earthiness of colostrum, of colostrum and vernix

and blood. I can't write about the lighting or give you anything close
to a time frame, but two of the nurses were named Sharon

and each of them told me, as I begged for an epidural,
you don't need one, *this is your birth and this is your labor, feel that* (the long

wait begun in late July nearly up). I wanted to keep detailed notes
about hazardous waste dispensers, my first try at aspirating

my baby's nose, about the breakfast of Cheerios and tea and French
    toast,
but instead these loosely woven undies one of the Sharons dubbed

"Madonna lingerie"—wear and toss—instead, the doula and my
    husband
walking me to the bathroom to get those panties on and off.

And I can tell you about the luxury, on a Friday night, of popping
two Ibuprofens, taking my first unfettered, unfetused shower in
    months,

but I can't remember much about that art on the third floor
where they made me walk and walk. All I can see is a cow

in the middle of a stream, on either side of her that blurry green of
    spring,
are two blue doors, one marked THE TRUTH, the other, EVERY-
    THING BUT.

My Newborn's

diurnal, definitely diurnal,
with no interest in the phases

of the moon, in the nocturnally
lucent night blooming cereus.

She's attentive, very attentive,
to the richness of seeds,

to miscommunications, never confusing
what's eaten with butter and jam

with "cat fight" *(crepe chignon)*, attuned
to the tricks of jewelweed. She's

most capable of metamorphosis,
as are ladles, swing sets, spathes.

In relation to me she's always skyward,
skyward like the popcorn flower and the trillium.

Her tongue, both tibias, hail from the era
of Rosie the Riveter, women named Garnet

and Hazel. She's fire, all fire, but also
tending toward cymose, cymose and lacy,

most fashionably a relative
of the crepuscular thick-knees. To be

beautiful on a dissecting table,
all she needs is a dung-rolling scarab

pinned to her pink and white onesie:
her gait will be my gait.

What Little Girls Are Made Of

Tapir, pure tapir—all wide,
delicious ass. Herbivorous

to the core, union of fly rod
and shad roe. After hiking all the way up,

then all the way back down Mount Kinabalu.
In the month of pastels, fluorescent pink grass.

As American as a forest fire enveloping
your god-given home on the range.

With wheat berry eyebrows, resides
in the batter of Proust's madeline.

Also of the sorrowful women of Durer.
Of cantaloupe rind, of gargantuan zucchini.

Of Athena—all brains from the get-go, over-
brimming, teeming, full of knowing

hare-bell from bluebell, every genus
and every species, all brushed up

on conifer know-how, reminding us
spruces have papery cones.

Of granite, with meteor shower
skin, her nose, when it sniffs,

pre- and just- rainfall, her voice
a synthesis of Ginsberg and Plath—

"A Supermarket in London," amalgam
of nasty boy love and honey,

Lorca chasing her down the aisles hissing
Bees! You must devote yourself to bees!

"Babies in the tomatoes," yes,
but also of baby tomatoes. Of those believing

the world held up by a turtle. She's
the Thinker, Ye Olde Tick Tock.

She's the patch of geraniums
in full throttle, all wrists and sucking fists.

She's what glows and glows.

Victoria's Secret

's no secret, only rolls and saddles, only handles, gravity
doing as gravity does. I know this because after sifting

through piles of 36 Cs and 38 double D's—the pink & frilly, the dark
    & shiny—
all I can tell you is so much snappable spandex, so much Lycra,

cups twisted like handcuffs in countries where no one speaks
of the right to remain silent. If there's a secret, it's lost on me, unless

it's knowing, if you need assistance, you can push a button,
& a woman will enter your room saying she's built exactly like you—

not full-figured, but entitled to breasts like two stiff dollops
of whipped-up whites. Tell her to bring you what held up

the lunar module, all that the jostling and bouncing.
Tell her maybe the secret's the stuff our galaxy's

been dishing up for eons, Newton's apples, what we've always
always known. Maybe we could all learn a few things

from Jupiter and Saturn, resembling, as they often do,
those glamorous, distant stars.

My Body will Run with the Weeds Some Day

—Charles Simic

I shall die in Paris, in a rainstorm, on a day I already remember ...
—Cesar Vallejo

Harried and scatterbrained.
Loopy, not lucid. Illogical,

whimsical, flimsy. Misplacing
my keys at every turn,

my uncrossed t's, my untucked
wine-stained tee. It won't

be dramatic: My Death.
Absentmindedly, I'll slam

a parked car, lose sight
of the road, hit the curb

and flip. Run a hard-to-read-
or-altogether-missing stop sign,

swiped to decorate a dorm room,
my lifesaver tacked to a light-pink-

paneled ceiling, though likely
I wouldn't have even read it,

even if she'd hadn't an inkling
to steal. No, my death won't be

like Cesar Vallejo's, but it will certainly
deal with distraction, with a certain

city, a certain surface gone slick,
an out-of-the-blue belt of wind

while crossing a bridge, but unlike him
I already don't remember

which day, which car, which wind.

About the Author

Martha Silano grew up in New Jersey and was educated at Grinnell College and the University of Washington. Her previous collection, *What the Truth Tastes Like*, published by Nightshade Press, won the 1998 William and Kingman Page Poetry Book Award. Her poems have appeared in the *Paris Review, Beloit Poetry Journal, Green Mountains Review, Fine Madness,* and various anthologies and journals. She teaches at Bellevue and Edmonds Community Colleges and lives in Seattle, Washington.

Acknowledgments

Grateful acknowledgment is given to the editors of the following
magazines in which these poems first appeared:

Bellingham Review "Ingredients," "His Favorite Color is Green"

Beloit Poetry Journal "Salvaging Just Might Lead to Salvation"

Caffeine Destiny "Cabbage"

Cranky "Tit for Tat," "If You Want a Girl to Grow up Gentle, Lace
Her Tight," "At the Sayres Park Rowing and Sailing Center, Lake
Washington, Seattle, "To a Giant Allium"

CrossConnect "I Never Wanted to Travel Through Time"

Descant "After Drinking the Orange Liquid for the Glucose Toler-
ance Test"

descant "I'll Never Be Dorianne Laux at the Laundromat"

DIAGRAM "What Little Girls Are Made Of"

Ellipsis "My Son Asks 'What's a Torrent?," "What a Piece of Work
is a Man"

Fine Madness "Crazy," "Low Tide Walk with Mary Grace," "Suite for
the Visiting Dead"

Folio "The Forbidden Fruit"

Gargoyle "Blue Positive"

Hanging Loose "My Man with his Fly Reel Eyes"

LitRag "Forgetfulness the Great Bronchial Tree from Which I'm
Swinging," "Picking a Name While Picking Blackberries," "While
He Naps," "Sprinklers of the Western World"

Nebraska Review "Four a.m."

No Tell Motel "Gravitas"

Poetry Northwest "Mother of Peace," "Define Medical Terminol-
ogy and Conditions Associated with Conception," "Getting
Kicked by a Fetus," "What They Don't Tell You About the Ninth
Month," "Song for a Newborn," "Traveler's Lament"

Prairie Schooner "My Words"

Raven Chronicles "This is Not the Last Poem about Pears"

Rhino "I Don't Know What I Want, Only that I'm Desperate for It"

Seattle Woman "Explaining Current Events to a One-Year Old"

Tarpaulin Sky "People Are Doing It as We Speak"

**

Sincere gratitude to the Seattle Arts Commission, the Virginia Center for the Creative Arts, and to the Dutch Henry Institute of Technology/Boyden Family for providing financial support to write and revise many of these poems.

**

"Explaining Current Events to a One-Year Old" also appears in *Red, White, & Blues: Poetic Vistas on the Promise of America*, Virgil Suarez and Ryan G. Van Cleave, eds. (University of Iowa 2004).

**

"The Forbidden Fruit" also appears in the *Contemporary Northwest Poets Anthology,* Oregon State University Press & Ooligan Press.

**

"Song for a Newborn," also appears in *Pontoon #6: An Anthology of Washington State Poets* (Floating Bridge 2003). "Getting Kicked by a Fetus" and "Explaining Current Events to a One-Year Old" also appear in *Pontoon #7: An Anthology of Washington State Poets* (Floating Bridge 2004).

**

The editors of Cranky nominated "Tit for Tat" for *Pushcart XXX*.

**

Brenda Miller, Editor-in-Chief of the Bellingham Review, nominated "His Favorite Color is Green" for *Pushcart XXX*.

**

"Four a.m." also appears on *Literary Mama* (literarymama.com).

**

"Picking a Name While Picking Blackberries" won first prize in *LitRag's* 1st Annual Blackberry Poem Contest.

**

"Define Medical Terminology and Conditions Associated with Conception, " "Traveler's Lament" and other poems won the 2001 Macleod-Grobe Prize from *Poetry Northwest.*

**

A shortened version of "I Don't Know What I Want, Only that I'm Desperate for It" appears on Seattle Metro Buses as part of the 2005 Poetry-on-the-Buses project.

**

Hats off to the Ruby Group: Erin Malone, Kary Wayson, Shannon Borg, and Anna Maria Hong. Without you there'd be far fewer poems.

**

A heaping plate of gratitude to the Klatchers: Molly Tenenbaum, John W. Marshall, and Cal Kinnear, who gave me advice, encouragement, and a place to always feel welcomed.

**

Thanks to those who read, critiqued various drafts, and/or advised on the arrangement of these poems: Sharon Bryan, Moira Linehan, Stacey Luftig, Kelli Russell Agodon, and the many I've forgotten.

**

I am especially appreciative of the wisdom, compassion, and patience of Dr. Rex Gentry.

**

Thanks to the National Poetry Series, Autumn House Press, and Silverfish Review Press for selecting this collection as a finalist in 2002, 2003, and 2005.

Printed in the United States
205370BV00001B/281/A

9 780974 326429